The BE-Attitudes

Live Life Approved by God

The Be-Attitudes
Live life approved by God

Copyright 2006 Sarah A. Keith

Unless otherwise indicated, Bible references
are from the New International Version.

Editor: Kit MacLeod

Email: info@sundayschoolnetwork.com

The Be-Attitudes
Live life approved by God

Lovingly dedicated to my husband, Bob.

I especially want to thank Elizabeth Nielsen
and the J.A.Y. Women's Bible Study Group
for their helpful insights.

And as always,
to my wonderful friend and editor,
Kit MacLeod, for your encouragement in ministry
and helping me write better than I do!

The Be-Attitudes

Live life approved by God

The Be-Attitudes
Live life approved by God

*"Have this attitude in yourselves which
was also in Christ Jesus…" Philippians 2:5 (NAS)*

Contents

The Be-Attitudes
Live life approved by God

The Be-Attitudes
Live life approved by God

Getting Started

These lessons are for personal Bible study or groups. In a group setting, I recommend that one person facilitate the discussion. To further enhance your study time, I suggest looking up the Bible references marked, "Read" from different translations. The discussion questions can be worked together or privately, and then discussed.

I hope you will make the Beatitudes your daily attitudes, so you can live your life approved by God and become the person whom God intended you to be. Jesus' eight declarations of blessing are absolutely life changing!

In His Loving Grip,
Sarah A. Keith

The Be-Attitudes
Live life approved by God

1

"I just can't get over it!"

Most of us, if not all of us, at one time or another have to deal with experiences in our past or current life that make us stumble in our faith or that cripple us emotionally. It could be something as severe as being physically or sexually abused as a child, or a feeling that our parents didn't give us the proper attention we needed growing up. Maybe it's a broken friendship or business plan gone sour, or a disappointment so deep that you can't get past it. Whatever "it" is, many times these painful experiences can affect us the rest of our lives, preventing us from reaching our greatest potential or eventually destroying us. Trying to "get over it" doesn't work. We try and fail, and "it" goes round and round in our minds, blocking us from receiving what God intends for us. Thankfully, there is an alternative. God can heal our pain, so we can live productive, God-approved lives.

The Be-Attitudes
Live life approved by God

If you feel powerless to overcome your pain, there is hope. You are about to discover that the Beatitudes are the key to unlocking your spiritual and emotional well-being, so you can "get over" the painful experiences in your life—past and present—and have hope for the future!

The Beatitudes are the eight declarations made by Jesus at the beginning of his Sermon on the Mount, recorded in Matthew 5:3-12. Each one begins with the words, "Blessed are," and continues with a statement concerning those who live in obedient and joyful unity with God. They are for those who partake in his salvation, and who have entered into his kingdom, not in its fullest sense, but as a foretaste of what's to come.

The word "blessed" is from the Greek word, "makarios," which means, happy, well off, or fortunate. Some Bible translations use the term happy, yet happiness most often depends on one's emotional state—it is temporary. On the other hand, blessed also means favored, which more accurately describes the spiritual harmony of a person who is in relationship with the King of the universe—it is eternal.

The Be-Attitudes
Live life approved by God

God's children are blessed because we are *approved by Him.* He has bestowed his favor on us, and given us a place in his kingdom (2 Corinthians 6:2)!

However, because we live in the "already and not yet" of God's kingdom, the Beatitudes teach us what it means to live here and now, they are concerned with our inner lives and attitudes. They teach us how to think and act and how to receive God's riches in order to become the salt of the earth and lights on a hill. They also tell us what rewards are in store for those who abide by them. The Beatitudes help us realize God's purpose and plan for our lives!

I confess that before embarking on this study, I had never closely studied the Beatitudes. I think I did what many people do, read them quickly to get to the "real meat" of Jesus' sermon. What a mistake that is, because unless you understand them, it is impossible to apply the rest of the sermon to your life.

Enjoy your study; you're about to discover how blessed and favored by God you truly are!

The Be-Attitudes
Live life approved by God

2

Blessed are the poor in spirit, for theirs is the kingdom of heaven. Matthew 5:3

Is being poor ever a good thing? Don't we all we want to be rich in spirit, rich in health, and rich in our bank accounts? We want the best of everything, because having the best is a measurement of our success—right?

When Jesus began his sermon on the mount by saying, "Blessed are the poor in Spirit…," he was not touting the benefits of those who *don't* have money, nice clothing, or fine food to eat. In God's economy, being poor in spirit is about emptiness—spiritual emptiness. It is coming to understand that we are powerless to help ourselves and that nothing in us naturally chooses to follow God's ways. Our condition apart from Jesus Christ is bleak:

The Be-Attitudes
Live life approved by God

"There is no one righteous, not even one; there is no one who understands, no one who seeks God. All have turned away, they have together become worthless; there is no one who does good, not even one."
(Romans 3:10-12)

And no matter how hard we try, or how good we become, we can never earn God's favor or approval:

"All of us have become like one who is unclean, and all our righteous acts are like filthy rags…"
(Isaiah 64:6)

Another way to say Jesus' opening statement is, "*Favored* or *Approved by God*, are the empty ones, for theirs is the kingdom of heaven." Being empty, or poor in spirit, is exactly what Jesus wants from us. By admitting our spiritual poverty we can begin to heal spiritually and emotionally.

Have you recognized your spiritual poverty?

The Be-Attitudes
Live life approved by God

Philippians 2:5-8 tells us exactly what God wants from us:

> *"Have this attitude in yourselves which was also in Christ Jesus, who, although he existed in the form of God, did not regard equality with God a thing to be grasped, but emptied Himself, taking the form of a bond-servant, and being made in the likeness of men. And being found in appearance as a man, He humbled himself by becoming obedient to the point of death, even death on a cross."* (Philippians 2:5-8 – NAS)

Think about this: Jesus had equal status with God, but he gave up all the privileges that come from being God to become a servant! Can you imagine this? Jesus set aside his God-self, his deity, to become a lowly human-being! He did this for one purpose: to redeem the sons and daughters of Adam and Eve, who *wanted* equality with God, "to be like God," and by trying to get it, disobeyed him.

Read: Genesis 3:1-7, 14-15.

The Be-Attitudes
Live life approved by God

Verse 15 of Genesis predicts the future for our adversary, and for us, "I (God) will put enmity between you (Satan) and the woman (Eve), and between your offspring and hers (Eve's ancestors); he (Jesus) will crush your head, and you (Satan) will strike his heel."

Jesus came to earth to redeem us, to buy us back. He emptied himself, he became nothing, he became a man, a slave, to save us from death! God wants us to do the same thing, *to have Jesus' same attitude*—to empty ourselves.

God's approval is possible only through Jesus' sacrifice. Satan struck the heel of Jesus when he was crucified—at the time, it appeared as if all was lost. But Jesus crushed Satan by overcoming death—he rose from the dead!

> *"Where, O death, is your victory?*
> *Where, O death, is your sting?"* 1 Corinthians 15:55

We are approved by God by following Jesus' example: *he did not seek equality with God, but emptied himself …*

The Be-Attitudes
Live life approved by God

The immediate benefit of admitting to God that we are poor in Spirit, and that we cannot save ourselves, is that he forgives *our* sins, fills us with his Spirit, and we become a heirs to his heavenly throne. We begin the journey. We are blessed—favored by God—because we have entered God's kingdom, but not in its fullest sense; that will come when we see him face to face.

"Let the poor man say, 'I am rich in Him.'"

The Be-Attitudes
Live life approved by God

Discussion Questions:

1) How would you define spiritual poverty?

2) What do the following references have to say about being "poor": Psalm 34:6; Psalm 40:17; 2 Corinthians 8:9; Revelation 3:17-21?

3) According to Philippians 2:5-8, what five Christ-like attitudes should believers possess?

4) According to Galatians 5:1, what happens when you don't empty yourself?

5) What blessings are in store for those who have admitted their spiritual poverty and are now filled with God's spirit? (See Psalm 84:10, John 15:1-5, Romans 8:35-39, Ephesians 1:3-8, 13-18, Hebrews 13:15.).

3

Blessed are those who mourn, for they will be comforted. Matthew 5:4

"My God, my God, why have you forsaken me?"
(Matthew 27:46)

As Jesus hung dying on the cross he cried out, *"Why… me?"* At that pinnacle moment the full wrath of God, which was meant for us descended on him; he became our sin offering (2 Corinthians 5:21).

When we mourn, we can feel like God has abandoned us. We cry out, "Why me?" Yet, Jesus knew why he came to suffer and die—he willingly went to the cross for the joy that was set before him (Hebrews 12:2). It may seem odd that Jesus found joy in suffering, but he knew his suffering had purpose. His death provided our forgiveness and restored our lives to the Heavenly Father.

The Be-Attitudes
Live life approved by God

Our problem is that we, unlike Jesus, usually don't know or understand why God has allowed pain and suffering in our lives. Oftentimes, it seems purposeless or cruel.

When we mourn, we need the supernatural comfort that only God can give. Jesus knows that living on earth can be very painful. He realizes that our hopes and plans get crushed, friendships are ruined, our loved ones die, and this breaks our hearts.

We mourn because the world is not right. Sin has corrupted the planet. There is pain and sickness, death, decay, and disease. The Bible says the entire creation groans in pain until the coming of Jesus (Romans 8:19). In fact, it is in the midst of our mourning where we come to understand how needy and poor in spirit we really are! (Psalm 18:6, 22:24, 84:2)

Let's look at two passages that speak to Jesus' mourning. The shortest and probably the most famous one is, "Jesus wept." He wept because one of his closest friends had just died.

Read: John 11:1-45.

The Be-Attitudes
Live life approved by God

Lazarus is dead and his sisters, Mary and Martha, are mourning his death. When Martha discovers Jesus is finally coming to help them, she runs out to meet him. Can't you hear her saying, "Why?" "If you had been here, things would have been different! I don't understand. You had the power to heal him! Why didn't you help us? Why did *you* let him die?"

Then Mary comes out to meet Jesus and wants to know the same thing, "Why?" "If only you'd have been here..." "If only you'd cared!"

Do you hear their desperate, heart-wrenching accusations?

We want to know the same things too. "God, why?" "If only you had healed my child." "If only you had given me parents that loved me." "If only *you* had cared enough to be here when I needed you the most!" "If only you had made me different from what I am." "If only..."

What is your, "If only?"

When Jesus heard Mary's and Martha's questions, he didn't accuse them for lack of faith. No, he cried too! But why did he cry? He certainly knew he would raise Lazarus to life in just a few seconds. He could have scolded the women, but he didn't. So why did he cry? It doesn't make any sense! However, it makes perfect sense when you realize he *does* care. He understands. He knows this wasn't how life was supposed to be. He cried with them. He mourned sin's destructive results and the pain and suffering it caused in their lives.

Read the second passage of Jesus' mourning in Luke 13:31-35.

"Oh Jerusalem, Jerusalem...how I have longed to gather your children together, like a hen gathers her chicks under her wings, but you were not willing..."

Do you hear Jesus' sorrow for Jerusalem? He mourned for something that wasn't to be. The tenderness of Jesus' words is contrasted with the starkness of their rejection of him: *they were not willing.*

We too mourn for hoped-for situations that will never happen, for relationships or plans that just aren't going to be. We must empty our hearts of mourning by pouring it out to God. Take time to mourn your pain, suffer your loss, and grieve your regrets; Jesus mourns with you. But be careful not to hold onto your pain and allow it to become an excuse for retreating from life. You just might be tempted to use your suffering to explain away your own shortcomings and sinful failures.

Have you ever thought, *"If this hadn't happened to me, then I could have been successful?" "If this hadn't happened, then I would be happy." "If this hadn't happened, then life would be different, and I would be different." "If these things hadn't happened, then I could trust God."*

But why does suffering take us by surprise? Where do we get the idea that if we pray enough and trust enough, then we'll be free from suffering? It could be a result of our western entitlement mindset, but it certainly isn't what the Bible teaches us. Think of Isaac, whose father held a knife over his head; or Joseph, who was sold into slavery. And of course there's Job, who lost everything: his children, his health, and his worldly possessions. What about Steven, Paul, Peter, and Jesus? Their lives ended in horrific ways. So why do we not expect to encounter the same? Is it false teaching or preaching that makes us think this way? Possibly, but maybe it's a remnant memory that God programmed into our hearts at creation, because it wasn't supposed to be like this. We *were* created to live pain-free, suffer-free, and mourn-free lives, but sin has corrupted our heritage.

Read Hebrews 11.

The Bible teaches us that Godly sorrow brings repentance that leads to salvation (2 Corinthians 7:10). The point of Hebrews 11 is not how these great people of faith suffered, but that they trusted God through their suffering. It would be grotesque to welcome pain and suffering into our lives, but it *is* necessary to expect it. God doesn't let us suffer out of cruelty. We suffer because we live on a corrupt planet, but it is also in the midst of our poverty and grief that we come to know our need of the Savior. *This is purposeful suffering.*

My pastor relayed the following story of one of his friends who went to the doctor for a check-up. The doctor asked him, "How are you getting along?"

The man replied, "What do you mean?"

The Be-Attitudes
Live life approved by God

"Your infirmity, your disease, how are you dealing with it?"

The man declared, "I don't see this as an infirmity. I see it as a blessing."

"A blessing? How's that?" the doctor replied.

The man continued, "Are you a Christian?"

"No."

"Well, I am. And I believe that God has allowed me to have this disease for a reason; so I see it as a blessing. In fact, because of this disease I have the opportunity to speak to people I wouldn't ordinarily have the chance to meet and tell them about Jesus; just like I'm telling you now."

What a powerful testimony! This man understands that, compared to an eternity with God and the glory to be revealed, his suffering is a temporary situation; it is purposeful! He is able to embrace God's comfort in the midst of his suffering.

Take an honest look at your mourning. What prevents you from trusting God? Pour out your tears and allow him to fill your void. God doesn't wait in anger, he waits in love.

The Be-Attitudes
Live life approved by God

The sacrifices of God are a broken spirit; a broken
and contrite heart, O God, you will not despise.
(Psalm 51:17)

Jesus warned us that we would have trials. God may reveal the purpose for our suffering, or we may never understand why these things happen on this side of heaven. Even so, Jesus promises to be with us and never leave us (1 Peter 1:6, Hebrews 13:5).

"Therefore also God highly exalted Him, and
bestowed on Him the name which is above every name,
that at the name of Jesus every knee should bow, of those
who are in heaven, and on earth, and under the earth,
and that every tongue should confess that Jesus Christ
is Lord, to the glory of God the Father."
(Philippians 2:9-11)

After Jesus suffered, God comforted him and lifted him up. In this beatitude, Jesus assures his children that when we mourn, we too will be comforted.

The Be-Attitudes
Live life approved by God

God sent his Son to redeem us from Satan's death-grip. He has a better plan for us than we do. While we live on earth, we can never be totally satisfied. In fact, we shouldn't get too comfortable here; this is a temporary situation. Our true home is heaven with Jesus!

Don't allow your trials to make you bitter; they have a purpose. God will use them to make you into the person he intended you to be. The comfort that Jesus promises is partially for here and now, but ultimately you will be fully comforted in the arms of The Hearer of Cries.

> *"God will wipe away all our tears and there will be no more death or mourning or crying or pain."*
> (Revelation 21:4).

"O Love that will not let me go, I rest my weary soul in thee."

The Be-Attitudes
Live life approved by God

Discussion:

1) Is there something you are mourning about or have mourned over in the past? How has this affected you?

2) Jesus tells his followers to take up their cross and follow him (Matthew 16:24-25). In light of this imperative, how are mourning and suffering to be expected in the lives of believers as they are being conformed into the image of Christ? (See also Isaiah 53:3; Matthew 5:39, 44; Luke 17:25; Luke 24:26 and Hebrews 13:1-3.)

3) Read Romans 5:1-5, 2 Corinthians 1:3-7, and Hebrews 12: 2-13. How do these verses give purpose to suffering?

4) Would understanding why you mourn or suffer make life easier?

4

Blessed are the meek, for they will inherit the earth. Matthew 5:5

Meek is not a word we often use to describe a powerful, self-assured person. The idea of meekness might even call up images of being mousy or weak, but that is the opposite of what it means to be meek. The Hebrew word for meek means to be humble or lowly, as a servant is in relationship to a king. On the other hand, meek in the Greek language means *powerful strength under control*. It is the idea of a wild horse that has been tamed and can now be controlled to serve a useful purpose. From these terms we learn that a meek person is one who *serves with controlled strength*, a person who doesn't have to be a servant, but one who is willing and able to accept his or her position under someone else's authority.

Jesus was meek. He was the living definition of power under control. As God in the flesh, Jesus emptied himself; he humbled himself and came to earth as a man to save us. Even though he had all the authority in the universe to do as he pleased, he became a servant. He subjected his position and chose to put it aside to rescue us. He obediently accepted God the Father's will for himself and did what was necessary to save us. He was willing to save us, but more importantly he was *able* to save us.

Because we sin, there is a death penalty judgment against us. Romans 6:23 says, "The wages of sin is death..." The Bible tells us that God requires a perfect, spotless sacrifice, one without defect, to pay for our sins (Leviticus 4:32, 17:11). Therefore, not just anyone could save us, but Jesus was *able* to save us, because he was perfect and without sin. Had he not been perfect, his sacrifice would not have been sufficient to pay our death penalty judgment.

Read: John 13:3-12.

What an awesome example of meekness Jesus gave to us! He also tells us that if we do these things, if we humble ourselves, serving others as he did, there is a blessing in store for us. God knows how he "wired" us. He knows we are happier people when we help others and are more concerned with other people's needs over our own.

The Be-Attitudes
Live life approved by God

Jesus has all power and authority, yet he uses sinful people to help build his kingdom. Meek people know *they can do all things through Christ who gives them strength (Philippians 4:13),* yet they are willing to ask others for help. Meek people are not self-absorbed and self-confident; they are Christ-absorbed and Christ-confident. Those who are meek in spirit are promised a great inheritance: to gain the earth, but what does this mean? To inherit means *to come into possession of or to receive as a right or divine portion.* But first and foremost, God's grace is a free gift. We don't earn anything from God; we are not entitled or have the right to his inheritance.

To inherit also means *to receive from an ancestor as a right or title.* The Bible says, "To all who received [Jesus], to those who believed in his name, he gave the *right* to become children of God -- children born not of natural descent, nor of human decision or a husband's will, but born of God" (John 1:12). Therefore, inheriting the earth is given as a divine portion for those who are God's children.

The Be-Attitudes
Live life approved by God

Meek people don't inherit the earth because they've earned it. None of God's gifts are earned or deserved (Ephesians 2:8-9). Meek people inherit the earth because they can be trusted with it. When we are following Jesus' example of meekness, our needs are set aside for the good of others, so that we have their best interest at heart.

Read: Philippians 2:1-5.

There is coming a day when God will establish a new heaven and a new earth; so take note, it will only be inherited and inhabited by God's people!

Are you *willing* to accept your position as a servant and serve God and others? Jesus did this for us; how can we not do the same for the King of the Universe?

Are you *able* to serve God and others? No one in his or her own strength is able, but God can *enable* his children to do whatever it is he has called them to do. You must first be willing, and then God's spirit will give you the supernatural power to accomplish the task he has in store for you.

The Be-Attitudes
Live life approved by God

Read: Philippians 4:13.

God can make you *willing* and *able*, but you must first recognize your spiritual poverty, *Blessed are the poor in Spirit…,* ask Jesus to be your Savior, and then ask him to make you able. This is not a one-time request; it is a lifelong process.

> *Now to him who is able to do immeasurably more*
> *than all we ask or imagine, according to his*
> *power that is at work within us.* Ephesians 3:20

The Be-Attitudes
Live life approved by God

Discussion:

1) Read Proverbs 3:5-6, John 1:12 and James 4:7-10. Before you can receive God's blessing, what must you do?

2) Read Matthew 19:14, John 2:13-16, John 10:17-18, 2 Timothy 1:7-9 and 1 Peter 5:1-7. What do these verses say about meekness?

3) Read Psalm 37:9, 11, 22, 29, 34; Isaiah 57:13 and James 2:5. What do these verses have to say about a believer's inheritance?

5

Blessed are those who hunger and thirst for righteousness, for they will be filled.

Matthew 5:6

What if we never grew hungry or thirsty? We'd have to force ourselves to eat and drink just to survive. Happily, or maybe unhappily for some of us, this isn't the case. When we're hungry and thirsty, most of us have no problem filling that need.

Jesus said we are blessed, and approved by God, when we hunger and thirst for righteousness. Desiring righteous living is not natural. We are born sinful (Psalm 51:5). If you don't believe it, just put two toddlers in a room with one toy and see what happens. We don't have to teach selfishness, do we? Hungering and thirsting for righteousness comes only after God makes us aware of our spiritual poverty, he then fills us with his Spirit. Only then will *our* spirits begin to feel the hunger pangs for righteousness.

The Be-Attitudes
Live life approved by God

Read: Genesis 15:6 and Romans 3:22

Jesus makes us righteous by his sacrifice on the cross; we receive his perfection, he takes our sin. It's the great exchange, and we are blessed, because, apart from Jesus Christ, it is impossible to hunger and thirst for true righteousness.

Read: Luke 15:11-24.

Righteous living is a life that conforms to God's will. In the parable of the Lost Son, the younger son realized his need only after he was hungry. In fact, it was a direct result of his emptiness and suffering that brought him to his senses. Only then was he willing to humble himself and admit his failure to his father.

Picture a potter pressing and shaping a lump of clay, forming it into his vision. He presses and pulls the clay, adding and taking away from the lump, until it takes on the form of what he has in mind for it to become. God, the Master Potter, is also in the process of shaping his people into what he wants us to be. His vision for our lives is to conform us into the likeness of his Son (Isaiah 64:8; 2 Corinthians 3:16-18)!

The Be-Attitudes
Live life approved by God

How do we know what God's will is for our lives? We begin by first knowing and learning what his Word says. It is there where God reveals himself to us, teaches us truth, and readies us for service.

All Scripture is God-breathed and is useful for teaching, rebuking, correcting and training in righteousness, so that the man of God may be thoroughly equipped for every good work.

(2 Timothy 3:16-17)

Read: Romans 12:1-2.

When we hunger and thirst for righteousness, we begin the process of being restored and perfected into God's image, making us able to serve God and determine his will for our lives.

God promises to fill us and satisfy us; yet, surprisingly the desire for righteousness is not quenched! In fact, the more we hunger and thirst for righteous living, the more we find ourselves wanting more and more of it! God satisfies us and fills us with himself, but as we grow closer to Jesus, we'll find ourselves hungering and thirsting for more and more of his righteousness. This is a miracle, and the evidence of a changed life!

The Be-Attitudes
Live life approved by God

Read: John 4:4-15; 7:37-38; Revelation 7:17.

Jesus wanted the woman to understand there was more to life than earthly needs and concerns, and that he was the answer to all her troubles.

Read: John 6:29-51.

The people wanted a sign as great as or greater than Moses and the manna given in the desert; then they would believe in Jesus. However, Jesus pointed out that the bread given was from God and not from Moses. Jesus wanted them to understand a deeper truth, that he, Jesus, was the true Bread sent from heaven, and that only in him would they be completely satisfied.

These water and bread verses are the keys to earthly contentment. Only in Jesus, by Jesus, and through Jesus do we desire righteousness, and are then satisfied—filled with God! It is entirely the work of the Spirit living within us that imbues righteousness.

As God controls more of our lives, the effects will be seen in the way we think, behave, and how we treat others. And not only will

The Be-Attitudes
Live life approved by God

we begin to desire righteousness for ourselves, we will long to see "right" done in our world.

Only when we let go of trying to control our lives, and allow God to be our God, will we find peace with Him and ourselves. Becoming conformed into the image of Jesus is not an easy process. It can be painful, but it is necessary.

Lord, you are the Potter, I am the clay.

The Be-Attitudes
Live life approved by God

Discussion:

1) Can you think of a time(s) in your life when your emptiness and suffering made you hunger and thirst for righteousness? Explain.

2) Romans 12:1-2 speaks of presenting yourself as a living sacrifice. What does this mean to you?

3) How does Jesus' sacrifice restore you to your original position of being made in God's image? (See Galatians 4:3-7 and Titus 2:11-14)

4) Read Jeremiah 18:1-6, Romans 8:28-29, Romans 12:2, and 1 Peter 1:14. What do these verses teach you about the purpose of conforming?

5) What does being filled with God look like? (Read Philippians 1:9-11; Ephesians 3:16-19; and Galatians 5:22-25.)

6

Blessed are the merciful, for they will be shown mercy. Matthew 5:7

Mercy is almost always linked with grace, but they are different. Grace is God's undeserved favor or kindness. It is a gift given by God and must be received through repentance and faith—turning from sin and trusting in Christ (Ephesians 2:8-9). Mercy, on the other hand, is kind treatment to those who are in trouble or need to be rescued from danger, and who may or may not deserve to be shown kindness.

Simply put, grace is *getting* what we *don't deserve*, God's gift of forgiveness; while mercy is *not getting* what we *do deserve*, God's punishment. But his mercy is more than that. When we find ourselves in desperate situations outside of our control, it is God, in his mercy, who rescues us.

The Be-Attitudes
Live life approved by God

Being merciful, like being righteous, isn't something that comes naturally. Mercy is learned. It is connected to the second Beatitude, *"Blessed are those who mourn..."*, because mourning can be our "Mercy Teacher." As we experience painful life events, we come to understand the importance of kind treatment from others. In fact, it is most likely during these difficult times that we discover more about God's love, faithfulness, forgiveness, and his mercy.

On one occasion in my adult Sunday school class we divided into small group discussions. One of the questions posed by the teacher was, "How have other people's responses to you during difficult trials helped you or hurt you?" One of the men in my group said that he really hadn't experienced difficult trials in his life, and he felt sort of bad or guilty about that (he was in his late forties). My response was, "Thank God. That is wonderful! Live on."

His experience got me thinking, though, of how important it is during trouble-free times to grow our spiritual roots. Our tendency is to forget about God when everything is going well, but this is the time when we must grow our roots down deep—through Bible study and prayer—so that when the storms of life come, and for most of us they do come, we'll have the power to stand firm in our faith.

The Be-Attitudes
Live life approved by God

Read: 1 Corinthians 15:58; 2 Corinthians 1:21-22.

Many people admit they grow more and learn more during difficult and trying times, than when everything is going along fine. In fact, this is one of the ways that God brings purpose to our suffering. Our suffering equips us to help others experiencing similar trials.

Read: 2 Corinthians 1:3-7.

This isn't to say that we can't be merciful towards others if we haven't been through the same situations. However, those who go through similar experiences are in a unique position to relate to another person's suffering more deeply, than someone who didn't go through the same experience.

Mercy is something we learn, but it is also a vow we must live into. My pastor and friend, Reverend Walter "Lucky" Arnold speaks of growing in our faith by living into our vows. Like the vows people take when they get married, Christ's followers must learn to live into their vows by faithfully serving God and others.

The Be-Attitudes
Live life approved by God

Therefore, when we make a confession of faith to God, admitting our emptiness and need of a Savior, and then promising to serve Him the rest of our lives, we must put mercy into action whether we want to or not, and whether we feel like it or not. We must live into it, because God demands we do (Luke 6:36). Most of the time we don't know what we're getting ourselves into, but God does; he promises to sustain us through every situation in life (Isaiah 46:4).

Read: Matthew 18:21-35.

Can you imagine behaving like the unmerciful servant in this story? It seems unbelievable, but this is what we tend to do. We have been forgiven of a much greater debt than the servant, yet we are prone to selfishness, envy, anger, and an unwillingness to help others. We are quick to be offended when others slight us, yet we expect God's mercy no matter how we behave. The judgment that Jesus pronounced in this story is frightening:

> *This is how my heavenly Father will treat you unless*
> *you forgive your brother from your heart.*

The Be-Attitudes
Live life approved by God

When we fully grasp that it is impossible to repay God for his grace and mercy shown towards us, it becomes exceedingly easier to forgive those who have hurt and offended us, whether they admit their shortcomings or not.

Since we have received God's grace and mercy, we are compelled, no commanded, to do the same for others.

If you want mercy, give mercy.

The Be-Attitudes
Live life approved by God

Discussion:

1) According to Ephesians 2:1-10 (esp. vs. 7 and 10) what is the purpose for God's extending his grace and mercy toward you?

2) How have you experienced God's mercy?

3) What does being merciful look like in your life? Has your own experience with suffering helped you to be merciful to someone else who is suffering? Explain.

4) According to Hebrews 4:14-16, who is your High Priest? How and when should you come to him?

7

Blessed are the pure in heart, for they will see God. Matthew 5:8

When I was a teenager I went to the Bahamas with one of my friends and her family. I'll never forget how crystal clear the water was. It was a blazing, azure blue that could have been two feet deep or two hundred feet deep. The water was so clean and pure you could see right to the bottom of the ocean floor! I couldn't wait for the boat to stop so we could jump in and swim. In contrast, years later my family and I went on vacation in South Carolina and swam at a nearby lake. The water was a dark, brown color. You couldn't see anything beyond an inch deep. No telling what lurked beneath. When given a choice, I think most people would choose to swim in the clean, pure water.

Many people when asked, "Do you think you're a good person?" will answer yes, because they compare themselves to others who they consider more sinful, or they don't understand how offensive their sin is to God. Choosing to have a pure heart is impossible apart from Jesus Christ.

This beatitude is closely related to the first one, *"Blessed are the poor in spirit."* We must first recognize our spiritual poverty and understand that nothing we have to offer God is pure or righteous—none of our thoughts, our intentions, or our decisions. God doesn't want us polluted and dirtied by this sinful world. He wants us to live lives that seek out pure living. Trusting in Jesus is the beginning point of having a pure heart, because at the moment we trust in Jesus, God fills us with his pure, Holy Spirit. Only then will we be able to *choose* pure living *and want it!*

> *…guard your hearts and minds. Keep your thoughts on things that are good, true and pure. Don't get dirtied by sinful things in this world. Live how God's Word has taught you to live. (Based on Philippians 4:6-9.)*

To guard our hearts and minds is a defensive position of protecting, shielding, or defending. But to be "on guard" is to watch defensively, to be actively alert to danger, on the lookout for any threat. The Secret Service is "on guard" when they're with the President, watching for anyone or anything that might harm him.

Likewise, the Bible tells us that we are to be "on guard" against the Evil One, because he is out to destroy us (1 Peter 5:8). We are in a spiritual, unseen battle against evil forces. We are to protect ourselves like warriors who wear armor in battle to protect themselves against their enemy.

I once took a fencing class with my brother. I had fun, until I actually had to fight him. I would begin in the "on guard" position, the stance a fencer takes to get ready to attack and defend, but each time my brother lunged at me with his sword, I would shrink back. Even though I was wearing protective gear, I could never muster enough bravery to face his attack. I knew he wouldn't show me any mercy!

Read: Ephesians 6:10-18.

When we face our Adversary wearing our protective gear, he will shrink back too, because Satan knows God will not show him any mercy either—he's doomed already. It's important to note that the armor pieces from the Ephesians 6 passage are all defensive protection, except for one, the Sword of the Spirit, which is the Word of God. It is our "on guard" protection against the Evil One.

The risqué topics on television and in the media that beam down into our homes are a stark contrast to what was acceptable only ten years ago. Even the subject titles on magazines, now prominently displayed on grocery store checkouts scream out their vulgarity. God wants his children to be "on guard" for a reason. He knows that when we allow trash into our lives, little by little the trash will seem more acceptable until we find ourselves like that proverbial toad in the scalding hot water. The water started out cool and gradually grew hotter and hotter until it boiled the toad to death. Don't be like the toad! Fill your mind and heart with God's Word, and he will direct your daily walk and lead you in paths of righteousness.

Being pure in heart begins the moment we trust Jesus to save us, but it is also a lifelong process of God conforming us into the likeness of His Son, *by obedience to his Word*. This battle is not fought alone; Jesus will see us through to the end.

The Be-Attitudes
Live life approved by God

In the Old Testament, the priests would have to purify themselves before entering God's presence. Today, when we clothe ourselves in Christ's purity, through his cleansing blood, we can come boldly into his presence, speak to him, and listen for the Holy Spirit's direction.

Read: 1 Thessalonians 5:21-23; Psalm 11:7; Hebrews 10:19-23.

As we live our lives in obedience to God and his Word, seeking and choosing his purity, he gives us the honor and privilege of participating with Him in advancing His kingdom and bringing his salvation and peace to others.

Lord, cleanse my life and make me pure!

The Be-Attitudes
Live life approved by God

Discussion:

1) Why do you suppose God wants his children to be pure in heart? (See Hebrews 1:9, Hebrews 9:14, Titus 3:1-8 and 1 Corinthians 3:16-17)

2) According to John 16:7-15 and Ephesians 6:10-18, how does God help to equip you to stay pure in heart?

3) According to 1 Corinthians 2:16, believers have been given the mind of Christ. This being the case, what responsibility do you think you have? (See also 1 Corinthians 6:19-20)

8

Blessed are the peacemakers, for they will be called sons of God.
Matthew 5:9

The Vietnam War raged on during my formative years. It was a tumultuous time with peace rallies, love-ins, and anti-war demonstrations held across the country. Thousands of peaceniks were calling for peace, but even the end of the war didn't bring immediate peace to Vietnam. Now the world faces another war, a war against domestic and foreign terrorism—enemies whose demands are not so easily defined, and whose borders are not so clear.

To our modern ears, *"Blessed are the peacemakers..."* may seem to be the most relevant of all the Beatitudes. In every generation we need peacemakers. Christians are called to bring peace to the world; we are to seek peace and pursue it (Psalm 34:14).

However, I don't think that is the point of this beatitude. In fact, Jesus says just the opposite, "...I did not come to bring peace to the earth, but a sword" (Matthew 10:34).

So what kind of peacemakers are God's children to be?

One of my New Testament professors, a dear man named Dr. Paul Caudill, made it a point to emphasize the connection between grace and peace when studying the Apostle Paul's letters to the church. Paul began his letters by writing, "Grace and peace to you..." In response, Dr. Caudill would always declare, "Without God's grace, we cannot have God's peace! God's grace *always* precedes God's peace."

Read: Colossians 1: 21; Romans 5:1, 9-10.

Think about this: if we are not "in Christ," then we are considered enemies of God. What a horrific thought! Who could stand if God is your enemy? No one, that's for sure!

But, if we are "in Christ," if we've received God's grace and his forgiveness, then there is no condemnation, no charge to bring against us (Romans 8:1). We are pronounced, "Not guilty," because through Christ Jesus, the Prince of Peace, the debt for our sin has been canceled (Colossians 2:13-14). We have peace with God; the war against him is over! We have rest for our souls!

Jesus came to bring peace between God and us (1 Timothy 2:5) and peace between one another. He is our Mediator. Once we've genuinely become grace and peace receivers, having become sons and daughters of God, the natural outcome, or I should say the supernatural outcome, is that we become grace and *peace* givers, sharing our faith with the faithless and the faithful.

Read: Philemon 1:6; 1 Thessalonians 5:9-16; Hebrews 3:13.

When we bring the message of God's grace and peace to our world by leading God's enemies to Jesus and strengthening the bond of peace between fellow believers, we have become true peacemakers!

But what about those troubling statements made by Jesus? *I did not come to bring peace to the earth, but a sword.*

The Be-Attitudes
Live life approved by God

Sadly, God's message of peace will not be received by everyone. For some, the very mention of Jesus' name will bring about disdain or outright hostility.

There is a conflict raging in our world between good and evil, between Jesus' followers and Satan's followers. This clash between believers and unbelievers extends into our families, our friendships, and our workplaces. Even so, we are instructed to make every effort to live in peace with everyone (Hebrews 12:14).

> *"Peace I leave with you; my peace I give you. I do not give to you as the world gives. Do not let your hearts be troubled..." ~ Jesus*

The Be-Attitudes
Live life approved by God

Discussion:

1) According to Jeremiah 6:16, Hebrews 12:14-15, Matthew 7:1-2, 1 Peter 3:8-12 and Proverbs 16:7 how are you to bring about peace in your life?

2) Has being a follower of Jesus resulted in creating conflicts in any of your personal relationships? Explain.

3) What does Colossians 3:12-15 say concerning how you should treat others, regardless of conflict, as a result of your faith?

4) What does it mean to be called sons "children" of God? (See John 1:12-13, Romans 8:13-16, Galatians 3:26-29 and 1 John 5:15.)

The Be-Attitudes

Live life approved by God

9

Blessed are those who are persecuted *because of righteousness*, for theirs is the kingdom of heaven. Matthew 5:10

Unlike the previous Beatitudes, this one is conditional. Jesus doesn't pronounce his followers favored for being persecuted for just *any* reason. He specifically says they are favored if they are persecuted *because of righteousness*.

I once had a friend who, after becoming a Christian, was wonderfully and obnoxiously zealous about his faith. Don't get me wrong, we should be zealous about our faith. However, his spiritual immaturity caused him to be less than tactful with his co-workers, and he often used his work time to witness when he should have been doing his work. As a result he was ridiculed for his faith.

The Be-Attitudes
Live life approved by God

"Blessed are those who are persecuted, *because of righteousness...because of me."* I've often wondered if my friend's co-workers treated him with scorn because of righteousness sake, or was it his approach and work ethic they found most offensive?

This Beatitude is a pivotal point for the rest of Jesus' sermon, because unlike the previous ones, which concern our inner lives and attitudes, this one is a blessing given to those who put those inner attitudes into action. Having admitted spiritual poverty, and being conformed into the image of Jesus, through the power of the Holy Spirit, Christ's followers—once empty, dirty vessels—miraculously become the salt of the earth and lights on a hill (Matthew 5:13-16).

Read: John 15:18-21; 2 Timothy 3:12-15.

When we live and act like Jesus, it is no surprise that persecution will come from those who are enemies of God. (Remember, those who are not "in Christ" are God's enemies.)

The Be-Attitudes
Live life approved by God

When I think of persecution, I think of the martyrs in the early church who refused to denounce their faith and chose to die instead. I also think of Christians in parts of the world today, where it is illegal to own a Bible or gather together with other believers to worship; they are being imprisoned and murdered for their faith. But Jesus says, "Blessed are you when people *insult you, persecute you* and *falsely say all kinds of evil against you* because of me" (Matthew 5:11-12).

Whatever form of persecution we may encounter, if it's because of our faith in Jesus, then we are considered favored and approved by God because of it! He is on our side; we can't lose! Rejoice, because great is our reward in heaven!

Read: Romans 8:35-39.

We do not battle alone. Jesus has prayed for us and the Holy Spirit pleads for us. Even when we don't have words for our prayers, the Holy Spirit knows how and what to pray for us. What a comforting thought! (Romans 8:26-39)

The Be-Attitudes
Live life approved by God

Read: John 17:1-24.

I love this passage from John! It is the prayer Jesus prayed right before his arrest and crucifixion. First, he prays for himself, then he prays for his disciples, and then he prays for all those who would eventually believe in him. He prayed for me, and if you are "in Christ," he prayed for you too! Jesus prayed for our protection from the Evil One (vs. 15). He prayed for our sanctification (vs. 17), the process of making us pure and prepared to see him face to face, and he prays that we would be united in our faith (vs.23).

Jesus is known as a man of sorrow and acquainted with grief. He knowingly faced persecution and death with the knowledge of the glory to come (Hebrews 12:2). He endured the cross for us; in this he found joy, because this gave us life and freedom. The way to glory for Jesus was through the cross. There wasn't a shortcut. If we, his followers, are to be conformed into his image, we must be ready and willing to do the same—there are no shortcuts—Jesus is our teacher!

Read: Luke 6:40; 1 Peter 2:19-21; 1 Peter 4:12-19.

The Be-Attitudes
Live life approved by God

Even when we fail at being salty, light-filled Christians, (and we will fail) God will not give up in conforming us into the image and likeness of his Son, because he has promised to never leave us or abandon us. (Hebrews 13:5)

As my pastor often says, "Jesus is coming again. In fact, he is coming in your lifetime! Either he will come for you individually in your death, or he'll come in the clouds for you and his people."

Will you be ready?

> *...Continue in your faith, so that when he appears you may be confident and unashamed before him at his coming.*
> (1John 2:28 paraphrased)

The Be-Attitudes
Live life approved by God

Discussion:

1) Jesus encountered persecution before he experienced glory. What ways are you experiencing suffering or persecution before reaching glory as defined by Jesus in Matthew 5:11? Explain.

2) The Psalms hold many promises for God's children in times of trouble. Read and comment on the following passages: Psalm 27:5; 31:14-16; 37:39-40; 46:1; 91:15 and 138:7.

3) What does it mean to let your light shine before men, and why should you? (See Matthew 5:14-16, John 13:34-35 and Ephesians 5:1-20.)

4) What does Isaiah 40:28-31, Galatians 6:9-10 and Hebrews 12:3 have to say about continuing in your service to God?

The Be-Attitudes
Live life approved by God

In closing, I hope this study has helped you to understand the importance of the Beatitudes for your life. I believe they hold the key to emotional and spiritual freedom and the healing that all of us so desperately need. I hope you'll put them into practice, so you will understand how blessed you are to be approved by God!

God's kingdom has begun; the new temple is being built, brick by brick and soul by soul (1 Peter 2:4-10). If you haven't started your Kingdom-journey, you can begin today by following *The Roman Road of Salvation*:

Romans 3:10 "There is no one righteous, not even one..."

Romans 3:23 "...for all have sinned and fall short of the glory of God..."

Romans 5:8 "God demonstrates his own love for us in this: While we were still sinners, Christ died for us."

Romans 6:23 "The wages of sin is death, but the gift of God is eternal life in Christ Jesus our Lord."

The Be-Attitudes
Live life approved by God

Romans 10:9-10 "If you confess with your mouth, Jesus is Lord", and believe in your heart that God raised him from the dead, you will be saved. For it is with your heart that you believe and are justified, and it is with your mouth that you confess and are saved."

Romans 10:13 "Everyone who calls on the name of the Lord will be saved."

Softly and tenderly, Jesus is calling,
Calling for you and for me;
See, on the portals He's waiting and watching,
Watching for you and for me.

Come home, come home,
You who are weary, come home;
Earnestly, tenderly, Jesus is calling,
Calling, O sinner, come home!

(*Softly and Tenderly,* Will L. Thompson, pub.1880)

Made in United States
North Haven, CT
29 April 2022

18714682R00040